the mundane

Poems by

Melissa Elder

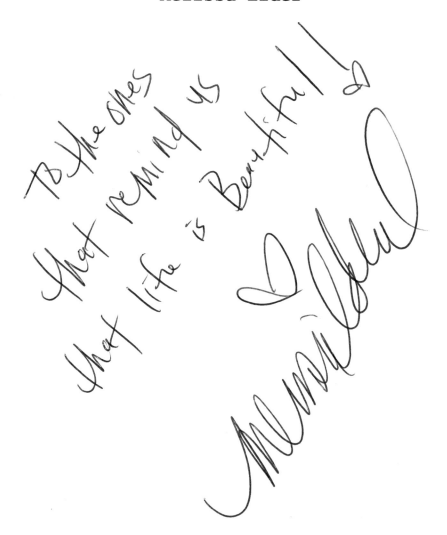

To the ones that remind us that life is Beautiful ♡
Melissa Elder

Copyright © 2022. M&B BOOKS LLC. All Rights Reserved. No reproduction of any content, including poetry or art, may be used without permission. For such permission, please contact:

M&B BOOKS LLC: Melissa.elder@live.com
Website: http://www.melissaelderbooks.com

Cover Design: Ryan Elder

Cover art and sketches by Susanna Maria Hackett / I Love You More Than Any Number, LLC.

For further information, please contact:
susannemaria@iloveyoumorethananynumber.com

All artwork is used in this book by agreement.

For those who are knee deep

in the mundane.

To rhyme or not to rhyme.

I like when poems rhyme.
I like when I can understand them.
But then I read poems from the Greats
and can't help but feel extremely juvenile
when I write a poem that not only rhymes,
but that others can understand.

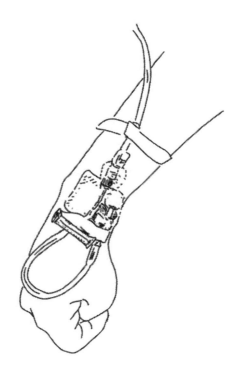

Labor.

She was mangled and sweated.
Her breath sharp and desperate.
Her hair was a nest of mess.

Her muscles were sore
and body broken.

But her eyes told a different story.
One of longing.
Of wanting.
Of waiting.
Of loving.

Birth.

Her face looked soft. So soft.
Cheeks flushed and pink.
Around her eyes, a calming contentment.
Her smile tired and reserved.
She looked at home.

How can someone look so peaceful,
I thought.

In her arms, a wrapped and sleeping baby.

The smell.

When she's born, she has a smell.
Unlike anything else.

Heaven still lingering maybe.

Hold after hold
kiss after kiss
hug after hug
cuddle after cuddle
her smell fades.

She starts to smell like us.

That's when I know that her smell can no
longer remind her of heaven.

The heavenly smell has faded,
and life begins.

Surrendering my heart.

My child.
My child, I surrender my heart to you.

It's no longer mine to toy with.
It's no longer mine to conspire with.
It's no longer mine to live with.

My heart belongs to you now.
From the moment I heard yours beat.

So please. I beg you please,

Hold it gently.

Normality.

I never in a million years
could have imagined
that my bad days
would consist of
checking my child's diaper
in front of other people
and finding poop
on my finger.

It goes fast.

"It goes by so fast",
they always seem to say.
"Savor every minute!"
While they go on their merry way.

Back to their homes,
so quiet and so clean.
No dishes in the sink
no toddlers to be seen.

I just stand there,
with my kids running wild.
Exhaustion in my bones,
holding a screaming child.

"But I'm so tired!!"
I want to yell at them.
"You just can't remember
what it was like back then."

The bags under my eyes
start to hang so deep.
I haven't brushed my hair
and I haven't brushed my teeth.

Will this ever end?
The constant sleepless nights?
Endless dirty diapers
or the sibling screams and fights?

And then right there,
as I'm knee deep in stress,
I hear my daughter ask

with flowers on her dress.

"Can I help you mom,
with anything you need?"
Her face so warm and kind
in her voice I hear the plead.

It stops me in my tracks,
I can't help but sit and stare.
"When did she grow up?
When did she start to care?"

And that's when I realize
that time does go by fast.
How do I savor this moment?
How do I make it last?

I stop everything I'm doing
and get down on one knee.
I hold her close to my chest,
And let myself just be.

I'll savor this minute.
I'll smell her hair.
I'll study her features.
I'll hold her so near.

Kisses.

I have her on my side,
while doing my daily chores.
Along for the ride,
as I'm sweeping these floors.

She makes a little coo,
I look at her plump lips.
I need her kiss so bad,
as she's propped up on my hips.

I ask her for "kisses",
she looks me in my eye.
She cups my face in her hands,
her mouth opens wide.

Our faces come together
with my lips puckered out.
Her kiss a bit wet,
milky drool, I have no doubt.

Although it was sloppy,
improved only with time,
it's the highlight of my day,
to feel her lips on mine.

Jekyll and Hyde.

I slowly open the door and see her standing in her crib.
Patiently waiting for me to pick her up.
She's smiling all over her face.
Giggling even.
I feel giddy to hold her.
I can't wait to hold her.
I giggle too.
I realize how much I missed her while she napped.
I pick her up and put my cheek next to her soft, red, post-nap cheek.
I can't get close enough to her skin.
I ask her for a kiss with her cheeks so soft and red.
She leans in and gives me a kiss so obediently.

I melt. I die. I might even cry.
She's perfect.

I take her downstairs with a skip in my step.
I put her down.
She points to something and makes a sound.
"What is it you want baby girl?"
I point to things to see if she'll nod.
No nod.
She starts to yell.
Reaching and pointing.
I try more earnestly to grab what she wants.
Nothing.
No satisfaction.
I start to panic.
"This? Do you want this?" I start to beg.
My voice with obvious desperation.
Her voice is getting louder.
Her yells turn to screams.

Loud shrieks of agony that hurt my ears.
I pick her up.
She slaps me and screams.
Now I'm angry.
She starts to cry.
Her cries are fierce.
Anger has taken over both of us.
She's screaming and slapping.
I'm frantic beyond rational thinking.

I hand her a cracker that was on the counter.

Silence.
She is silent.
Happily wiping away her tears.

I sigh with relief.

All I can think of is "when the devil is her next nap?"

Home.

For what is a home?
But a mere place
to rest my heart.

It need not be anything more.

"What do you do?"

"What do you do all day?"
He asked with his slicked back hair,
and tailored suit.
Grinning condescendingly.

I looked down at my sweats.
My hair slicked back in grease.

My pride up in flames.

I thought for a moment about what I do all day.
Me, a stay-at-home mom by choice.

I thought about waking my girls up with a kiss.
I thought about making new recipes.
I thought about long, hot showers.
I thought about reading a book.
I thought about walking in the mountains with my baby strapped to my chest.
I thought about lighting living room candles.
I thought about playing the piano.
I thought about noon day sex with my husband.
I thought about discovering a new park.
I thought about sledding in the snow.
I thought about being lazy.
I thought about being productive.
I thought about fall leaves crunching.
I thought about laughing with my friends.
I thought about trying new restaurants.
I thought about planting spring flowers.
I thought about dancing in the kitchen.
I thought about opening the curtains.
I thought about walking my daughter to school.

I thought about writing poetry.

My eyes looked up at the man,
while grinning condescendingly.

"I do whatever I want."

Unlearning.

One thing
I've learned
from adulthood

is the need to
unlearn some things
from childhood.

Motherhood is not.

Motherhood
is not a duty.
It is not oppression.
It is not an obligation.
It is not soul sucking.
It is not an identity.
It is not a must.

It is simply a choice,
and one where beauty can be found.

A rose.

The rose,
much like the woman.

So velvety.
So stunning.
A vision to behold.

But try and hold her down
and she'll make you bleed.

Doing It.

"It doesn't take much,"
the ignorant might sigh,
unaware of the pain,
because they've never dared to try.

It doesn't take much?
Just a daily sacrifice.
Running for my life,
and not thinking twice.

Dedicating every minute,
pushing myself every mile.
Constant sweat on my brow,
shoving down all the bile.

It doesn't take much?
To train all day?
Bruising my weary bones,
aches that don't go away.

Repeating all the mantras
that I've memorized by heart.
To get me past another minute,
further away from the start.

So, to you it may not seem like much,
for all you see are the smiles.
But inside I'm fighting desperately
to run these endless miles.

All they see.

I have to laugh at all the people
who look at parenthood and only see

stinky diapers
loud screams
boogers
messy hair
fighting
dirt
scrapes
late nights
crying
sore nipples
stretch marks
wrinkles
weight gain
balding
hitting
chasing
yelling
sighing
no free time
screen time
early mornings
exhaustion

Because they're dead right.
Except for the part where love overrides it all.

What love is to me:

Love to me,
is saving the best parts
of my personality
for the people
who matter
the most.

The struggle,
is to decipher the people
in my daily life
who matter
the most,

and to love them.

Love.

"Mom what is love?"
She so innocently asked.
I sat and thought about this
while finishing up my task.

She asked me again,
with my face in a stare.
How can I possibly answer
with how much that word bares?

How can I answer
that it's out of my control.
The love I feel for her
Overtakes my entire soul.

Or when I look at her sister
a wrapped gift from God.
A perfect child freely given
to a mother so flawed.

Or when I look at dad
I don't just see a man.
My life to him I've given,
my body, my heart, my hand.

I look down at her
as she patiently waits.
I want to tell her everything
but for now, all I can say

is that "love is simple.
It's a feeling from inside.
You'll know when you feel it.

The smiles are hard to hide."

She looks down from me
and I can hear her mind go.
And then just like that
I see the smile start to grow.

"Oh, I see" she says,
"I know exactly what love is.
Love is when I help my sister,
and then she gives me a kiss."

Staring out the window.

"What's the point?" she thought
as she sat and stared.
Out the window in her kitchen,
with all the city lights flared.

Everything I do,
gets forgotten anyways.
Everything I accomplish
will get zero praise.

It appears the days
are all for naught.
Everyone moves on,
and I'll be forgot.

Why do I bother
with these menial things?
These tiny little chores
that add up to nothing.

I want to be someone
I want to soar
I don't want to be forgotten
I want to be more.

But how can I do so
with this life so mundane?
How can I escape
this never-ending train?

Then I feel a tug
on my shirt from behind.
Startled from my thoughts

her soft blue eyes I find.

The reason I do it.
The very reason I stay.
The love I feel for her
gets me through another day.

Split.

Am I my child's
greatest bully?

Or my child's
greatest advocate?

Sometimes
it's hard
to tell.

Precious.

I've noticed as I get older,
I use words like "precious" and "tender"
and "beautiful" and "unbelievable."
Words that I thought as a child,
were only used by the old.

I understand now.

I understand now how precious time is.
I understand how tender a child can be.
I understand how beautiful a heart can really shine.
And I understand how unbelievable the world around me
truly is.

Infertility.

Infertility
is like not getting an
invite to the best party
in the world
that you were told
you were supposed
to go to.

Agony.

Where a mother's love
is planted at their birth,
equal is her agony
planted at their death.

Benefiting

I'm imagining for one minute
that every single experience
I've ever had
in my life thus far,
is for the soul purpose
of helping someone else.

What does it mean to be a good person?

I look around my home,
and I wonder,
to be a good person
would I have to sell everything
and give the money to those who
need it more than I do?

Or does it mean
to simply be grateful
for the things
that I have
despite needing them or not?

Dark corners.

I have poison lodged
in the darkest corners of my heart.
It lingers
and it simmers.
I can feel it.

How do I rid this tar
from my heart?
I want to live.
I want to thrive.

I don't want these dark shadows
robbing me of the happiness
to be had in my every day.

This isn't who I want to be.
This isn't how I want to live.

The devil may try.

Is it possible to have everything?
I ask the devil on my shoulder.
He responds quickly with a "yes."

He mentions
the things that I long for;
the money, the house, the dress.

I feel envious
of the people I know
that have everything he has said.

My greed gets deeper,
my desire gets stronger,
my eyes now only see red.

Then out of nowhere
my shoulder angel whispers,
"my dear, you have everything already".

"You have girls who giggle,
a home so warm,
a husband whose love is so steady."

An image of my girls
comes quickly to my mind,
of each of them laying by my side.

One of them is laughing
while the other one jokes,
the thought makes me smile so wide.

Another thought comes

just as quickly as the other,
of my husband rubbing my back.

He knows that I've had
a very long day,
he's kindly trying to help me relax.

Now I'm sitting so still,
thinking of all that I have,
smiling, as I reminisce.

I'm feeling ever so grateful
for what I've been given
wishing everyone in the world could feel
this.

Quiet, simple prayers.

My dearest Heavenly Father.

Thank you for my beautiful family.

The very reason for which I live.
The very reason for which I exist.

I love them.
Oh, my goodness, I love them.

Please let me keep them forever.

And sorry for yelling at them today.

Gracefully aging.

At first, I notice all the age spots,
and then the wrinkles start to set in.
I sit and try to remember
what I actually looked like back then.

Face smooth as glass,
muscles visible on my arms.
Abs pulled in tight,
my body nothing but youthful charms.

I don't recognize this body
that I'm staring at right now.
I don't even know when it changed.
I don't even know how.

I look down at my stomach
stripes, blotches and sags.
I shake my head in disbelief.
I have nothing left to brag.

I look back at my face,
lines deep from my eyes to my hair.
Cheek bones starting to droop just a bit,
I start to wonder if I ever cared.

I think of all the laughs I've had
every single day.
To make these lines so visible,
to make them want to stay.

I think of my babies first home,
as I touch my battleworn torso.
I think of carrying them so close to my heart,

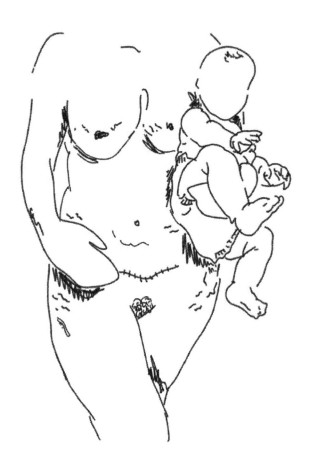

I think back to feeling them grow.

I think about my toes in the sand,
smiling, looking up at the sun.
Not caring that the spots on my face are being formed,
just listening to my kids having fun.

I start to smile while looking at this body.
These marks that show my past.
These visible signs that life has been good,
I wouldn't trade them for anything if you asked.

Beauty.

It's one thing to be naturally beautiful.

But it's another thing entirely
for your partner
to make you feel
naturally beautiful
even though you're not.

My body.

For most of my life,
I have despised,
berated,
critiqued,
shamed,
hated,
made fun of,
blamed,
and mocked
my poor, precious body.

I think it's about time I loved it.

Becoming a woman.

I've officially lost
count of all the
places on my body
that need shaving
before leaving my house.

Mobile.

It's the poison that feeds us.
It's the drug that soothes.
It's the connection that's needed.
It's the distraction that feels.
It's the reason for living.
It's the curse at our children.
It's the start of insecurity.
It's the end to living.
It's the hope that is lost.
It's the smile from a distance.
It's the bond to humanity.
It's the calming in the storm.
It's the guilt in our conscience.
It's the ignorance of rudeness.
It's the trigger for Xanax.
It's the persuasion that's not needed.
It's the need for therapy.
It's the desire to run away.

It's the damn phone.

Believing in God

"Why do you still believe in God?"
She asked.
"Is it not the same as still believing in Santa Claus?"
She spoke.

I thought about it for a moment.
I thought of these two faith provoking figures.
I thought of the comparisons.

"I guess by choosing to believe
in God there has been more positivity in my life.
More peace.
More love.
More hope.
More joy.
Very much like a child on Christmas,
the happiness is real."

To serve.

It's real nice to think of someone
and wish them
well.

But it's real love to
be the person to
make them
well.

A delicate flower.

If these delicate
little dainty flowers,
with their petals
near translucent,
can survive the winds
and harsh rains;

then surely,
I can too.

Within her a soldier.

She didn't know
all that it would take
to prove to herself
that she wouldn't break.

No one could hear it.
The fight was her own.
They couldn't feel the aches
in her mind, heart, and soul.

But what they could see
was a woman to behold.
Pushing only herself
to limits untold.

They could see a woman
and what she has done.
Overcoming herself,
her own battles won.

Within her born a soldier
as she pushed and as she cried.
For the only reason alone,
was to say at least she tried.

My Pride.

At first, I deny it happened.
Next, I'll try and blame them.
After that it starts to fester,
and I'll feel the anger grow within.

I'll turn to every angle,
until my wrong feels right.
I'll convince whoever I need to
to not give up this fight.

I'll chase after peace all day.
I'll run until I cry.
I'll stew into the late hours.
I'll search and wonder why.

I'll easily get upset
for what doesn't go my way.
I'll justify 'til I'm blue in the face,
it doesn't matter what you say.

And then just like that the fight is won.
Peace is felt again.

I feel like I can breathe.
I feel like I am sane.

All because of two little words,
"I'm sorry" so simple and pure.
Raw humility is all that's left,
Pride's only lasting cure.

Busy.

I never want to be too busy,
where I can't stop
and notice how
busy others are,

and have the time
to help them.

Feminism.

Can I still be
a passionate feminist
even though I'm
a white,
heterosexual,
cisgender,
stay-at-home mom,
with little college education,
who still believes in God?

K, cool.

Having a friend.

It's lovely to have a friend.

But it's life changing
to have a friend
that feels like home.

Wet hair.

She walked into
the restaurant with wet hair
and no makeup.
She immediately apologized
for not looking great.

I sat and smiled at her.

All I saw was a woman
who respected me
enough to be on time.

Who cared more for me
than the way she looked.

I saw a real friend.
And what real beauty looked like.

All for a measly pound.

I'll weigh myself.
I'll skip breakfast.
I'll clean harder.
I'll avoid lunches with friends.
I'll avoid holidays.
I'll run until it hurts.
I'll sweat until I'm soaked.
I'll drink myself drown.
I'll weigh myself.

I'll suck in my stomach.
I'll carry all the groceries at once.
I'll flex my butt while driving.
I'll park farther away.
I'll eat as slow as I can.
I'll lose sleep.
I'll compare every limb.
I'll weigh myself.

I'll make a salad.
I'll order another salad.
I'll eat salad after salad after salad.
I'll avoid the mirror.
I'll berate myself in guilt.
I'll exercise while sick.
I'll wake up too early.
I'll covet other bodies.
I'll weigh myself.

I'll think back to what I ate.
I'll think about what I'm going to eat.
I'll take the stairs.
I'll stare at the dessert.

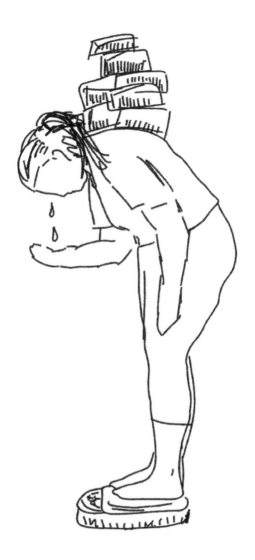

I'll smell the butter and sugar.
I'll pray for restraint.
I'll reset rules.
I'll weigh my food.
I'll weigh myself.

I'll read about tips.
I'll avoid happiness.
I'll write down each bite.
I'll avoid contentment.
I'll set the goals.
I'll avoid satisfaction.
I'll set my alarm.
I'll weigh myself.

I'll do whatever it takes.

To lose that pound.

Note: This poem was inspired by every person who's mentioned to me what it takes to lose a pound.

Real Women.

There's nothing more
refreshing
than being with women
who remind me
that I have more to offer
than the clothes I wear
and what I look like.

A sister.

She laughed with her.
She listened to her.
She spent her precious time with her.
And because of that,

Life was better.

The people pleaser.

She's often fighting
grappling
yearning
and working tirelessly
to please those around her.

The crime is not that
She pleases.
The crime is that she's
unaware of what pleases her.

Sadness.

He's been lingering.
Not close by,
deep down.

But something happens suddenly.
A word. A conversation. A reminder.

He's nearby.
I try to pat him down.
I try to keep him calm.
I try to hide his presence.

But he stays this time.
He's here.
He's not going down.
He's not going away.

I curl up.
I let myself feel him.
I let myself go.
I embrace him.

With the tears that won't stop,
and the flood of everything I feel,
he's relentlessly hovering
over every part of me.

The tears start to calm.
I feel my body lighter
after holding on so tightly.

I feel freed from the sadness
I've kept locked down for so long.

I let him go,
by giving in.

Conversations with a type 1 diabetic

"My grandpa died of diabetes."
"Does that hurt?"
"I thought you can't eat sugars."
"Is that worth a limb?"
"Are you going low?"
"Why are you tired?"
"My sister died of diabetes."

"Is it hard?"
"Tell me when you're going low."
"You need to stay on top of it."
"Do you need a juice?"
"You probably shouldn't eat that."
"My uncle died of diabetes."

"Are you scared for your kidneys?"
"Think of your girls."
"Are you checking your blood?"
"It can feel like a slow death."
"Everyone's diabetic."
"My mom died of diabetes."

"Are you taking care of yourself?"
"How is your husband doing with it all?"
"Have you seen 'Steel Magnolias'?"
"Why do you have so many bruises?"
"You should warn people when you give yourself a shot."
"My neighbor died of diabetes."

"You seem like you're doing great."
"How many carbs can you have?"
"Is that why it was hard to have kids?"
"Maybe you should check your blood."

"Are you able to still do things?"
"My brother died of diabetes."

"Are you scared you're going to die?"

Secrets.

In life there are secrets.
Secrets that we keep.
Close to our hearts,
that run so deep.

Secrets that we fear
should never be said
out loud on our lips,
not until we're dead.

But what happens
when vulnerability wins?
When what's escaped?
All that's held within.

Someone sees us,
for who we really are.
Someone sees us
with all our scars.

No excuses to be said
just standing there bare.
Hoping they won't judge,
hoping they won't be scared.

But something happens,
completely by surprise.
They see themselves in me,
while looking in my eyes.

They feel compassion,
and empathy starts to grow.
My shame disappears

as their love starts to show.

We connect in ways,
that would never have been possible.
We share the same feelings
and growth feels hopeful.

So why do we keep
these secrets that run deep?
When we are all the same,
you and me.

A lust for humor.

You won't win me over
with flowers,
chocolates or gifts.

Bring me to tears
with laughter,
and I'll sink right in.

Personality.

I have found that
the personality
is the true face.

Our physical face
has very little to do
with what is ever seen.

Sadly, my make-up bag
tells a different story.

Little devils.

I never know if
the little devil on my shoulder
always gets the better
of me,

or if my little angel
just happens to be
as crude as I am.

Experienced.

You would think after so many years
of being a human being,
that I would be somewhat good at it.

Unfortunately, most days,
that's not the case.

Feeling a gust of gratitude.

In life there are peaks and valleys.

I'm finally standing on
what feels like the highest peak.

Most often I am crawling,
hands and knees
through sharp rocks,
dark skies,
treacherous valleys,
and noisy canyons.

From the peak I can only go down.

But my gosh,
the views are so beautiful
from where I stand.

And that sun feels
so warm on my face.

If there's no peace.

If there is no
peace in
my life,

then I can
at least
try to laugh
at the chaos.

Being alive.

There's a big difference
between being awake
and being alive.

Being awake my eyes are open.
My body is in motion.
I'm breathing.

But being alive is taking advantage
of the colors I see with my eyes.
Running freely until my chest burns.
Feeling others happiness and pain with them,
and laughing until I can't breathe.

Just because I'm awake,
Certainly, doesn't mean that I'm living.

My refuge.

There's no greater place
to rest my troubled heart
then in the escapes
of a good book.

Burdens.

I heard of another
school shooting
today.

I look down at my pile of laundry,
once a burden to me.
Now a safe place
to rest my fallen tears.

Mom.

In childhood there were very few things
that felt as safe and consistent,
secure and comforting,
soothing and centered,
then as to walk through the front door
every day after school
and hear my mom call out to me,

"I'm in here."

Dad.

His jokes were the backbone
to my childhood.
His attention was the confidence
of my teenhood.
His tight hugs are the warmth in
my adulthood.

Divorce.

Looking into these two caskets
that are open and full.
Two bodies lying lifeless,
expressionless and dull.

Vulnerable and exposed
to all the passersby.
Never making eye contact
to all those staring eyes.

"Did you hear what happened?"
They say, to every ear.
Not noticing the children
who are standing right there.

"Did she lose her mind?"
They'll say with disgust.
"Did he know that she was someone
that he couldn't trust?"

The gossip in tidal waves
ruining pride to be had.
Another story to them,
someone else's mom and dad.

As the kids stand around
these open caskets, with tears.
Thinking back to their lives,
thinking back to all the years.

Years with open hope.
Years so stable and kind.
Years with open laughter,

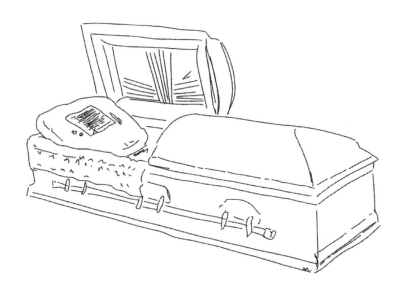

parents who took the time.

They can't comprehend
that their parents' marriage is dead.
The future so unknown,
all the security shed.

If only these types of deaths
were viewed as the real thing.
Flowers lining the sidewalks,
dinners inspired to bring.

If only people could see
that divorce is a death inside.
Our lives still in motion,
but our foundation is what died.

What remains with us
are the tender hearts survived.
Empathy engraved deep in the bones
for those who are still alive.

Tornados of Gossip.

Sometimes I feel like I'm
stuck in the middle of a tornado.
Stuck in the "he said, she said" spiral.
Stuck in the "did you hear" and "can you believe" whirls.

I keep thinking I'll eventually
get thrown out of this tornado
and land on solid ground.
That I'll be able to sit and watch
this tornado of gossip leave
and go to another field
while I sit peacefully on my land
finally rid of the spinning and swirling.

That day never seems to come.

I'm dizzy
from the
whiplash.
I'm dizzy
from the
noise.

Am I stuck because I don't know how to
let go and ride these violent winds?
Or because I don't think I'm strong
enough to throw myself out?

What is betrayal?

Is it ego?
Is it heartache?

What causes the sting?
Why in the moment,
does it feel made for me?

How do I let go?
Does it burrow under my skin?
Does it find a home in my mind?

Is it possible to move on
when the damage is done?
When I'm left feeling bitter
and patience is all gone?

What is anger?

What causes the pain?
Is it rooted in my body?
Is it living in my mind?

Why does it hurt?
Does it start with pride?
Or end with it?

Let go.

There's so much
more room for life,

by simply letting go.

Dawn.

The sun has barely woken up.
It's quiet and calm.
Almost too calm.
The world still wants to sleep.

I step outside
and breathe in the air.
So crisp.
So delicious.

I think to myself,
this is my coffee,
what mother nature provides.

I feel my heart start to beat.
I feel ready to start this day.

Open road.

Who built these roads
so smooth and so black
letting me drive
without looking back

Who carved a road
in these thick, tall trees
so I could stand in their midst
and feel this quiet peace

Who dusted this sand
in this dessert so dry
with the cactus so tall
and the endless blue sky

Who used their hands
to chip at these roads
straight to ocean cliffs
where time is slowed

Who used their strength
and their precious time
to make these roads
that feel like mine

They curve straight to the top
of this mountain so grand
where I can see the world
right where I stand

They bring me to places
that I only see in my dreams
these endless smooth roads
these manmade streams

Dancing on Mountain Tops.

We hiked to the top
and not a soul was in sight.
So, we hit the "play" button
and danced into the night.

We danced for friendship
for life and for fun.
We danced to remind us
that we are still young.

We danced at the views
with all its twinkling lights.
We danced to let go
of all the daily fights.

We felt so alive
in that brisk, mountain air.
So close to the stars
without a single care.

Mountain air.

The air really is different up here.

So fresh and smooth.
No wonder these flowers can't wait to come alive.
I breathe it deep into my soul.

It cleanses the toxic inside me.
It lifts the load off my spirit.
It drowns my negative thoughts.
It invigorates my tired mind.

I feel purified from this mountain air.

I see the majesty around me.
The simple beauty in the details.
No judgement or critique.

I hope to bring it back with me to the city.

I exhale all that I want to leave behind
and I whisper "thank you" into the wind.

For the air really is different up here.

God is a gardener.

We head down South
to chase the sun,
and walk the desert sand.

We hike the trails
and climb the rocks,
it's a hot and barren land.

With no water to be seen,
and no vegetation around,
I wonder how anything grows.

But then I see
ahead on the trail,
a little color that shows.

I walk up to it,
and there at my feet,
are purples, pinks and blues.

The prettiest flowers
I've ever seen,
growing down in the cracks by my shoes.

I wonder how this
could possibly be,
with no rain or rivers that flow.

And then I smile,
thinking of God,
for only He, the Gardner, knows.

Spring.

I feel very similar to spring
you know.

Reaching as hard as I can
to pull my head out of the
dirt to feel that sun
on my face.

To feel alive again
after a long cold winter.

Summer.

The windows are all open,
the sun wakes us up.
No plans for the day,
no schedule or makeup.

We put on our swimsuits
and grab our friends.
We head for the water,
until the day ends.

They swim in the lake
they dig in the sand,
they catch the minnows,
their cheeks so tan.

They stop to eat oranges,
and peel them fast.
Juice drips down their chins,
it reminds me of my past.

I was young like them,
before real life began.
Time didn't exist,
I spent hours in the sand.

It makes me smile,
watching time travel.
Being with them,
as childhood unravels.

These are the days,
they will look back on,
with nothing but play,

from dusk until dawn.

This is summer.
This is being a child.
This is living, free, happy, and wild.

To catch a firefly.

To catch a firefly
and watch it glow
in your hands,
reopens the part of your brain
that once held the magic
of believing that unicorns run wild,
that fairies fly in the forest,
and that rainbows still hold
the pots of gold.

Fall.

I look out the window
and see the trees sway.
The cool northern breeze
is calling me by name.

I open the door,
and feel autumn on my face.
It's cold. It's awakening.
It's scrumptious to the taste.

I hear leaves crunch
I see the colors turn
to orange, yellow,
and reds that burn.

I throw on my wool sweater,
and step through the door.
I need to be outside,
it's what Fall is for.

East Coast.

Spring is
renewal

but

Fall is
religion

Winter mornings.

It's 5:30 am
and she's already up.
I'm half asleep
while I pick her up.

It's snowing quietly outside
and still pitch black.
So, I make myself some tea
and lay her in my lap.

I wrap the blanket around her
and go light the fire.
Whoever wakes up this early
I can't help but admire.

I nuzzle in next to her
as tired as can be.
She points to a book,
her favorite one, I see.

I go over and grab it,
I hope she'll start to drift,
but as I read aloud
her mood starts to shift.

She perks right up,
with her story being read.
And all I can think about
is going back to bed.

She leans into my side,
and wraps her arm around my chest.
I look at the falling snow,

and start to doubt I need more rest.

Reading to her
by the fire feels so cozy.
I guess there are some perks
for waking up this early.

The man with little words.

To the man with little words,
but smiles all the same.

His spirits always high,
always up to play the game.

Shows up when he's asked,
does more to please, than say.

For there's no need to chat,
when your actions are what stay.

Marriage.

Why, yes you can
have all of me.

But only if you
allow me to change
everything about
myself.

Fighting.

I once believed
that the fights
that held the most damage
were the dramatic Broadway shows
of slamming doors,
screaming,
yelling,
and crying.

Now I know that the
deep sea of silence
is where the heart
slowly
stops
beating.

Boomerang love.

It took me getting away
to feel closer to you.

Forest floor.

The rain was light on the leaves.
The sound incredibly therapeutic.
The moss was thick and soft.
Better than a duvet
in my humble opinion.
The smell of the fresh rain
was euphoric and invigorating.
The tree trunk was strong and sturdy,
the headboard that was needed.
My hair dripping wet.
His breath heavy.

A scenario that I couldn't have
dreamed of even in
my wildest imagination,

for the best date.

Getting away.

We plan a trip,
to get away from them.
To talk and cuddle,
and finally sleep in.

We eat out,
we play around.
We watch movies
we hit the town.

But after a while,
of doing what we want,
we start to notice,
while eating our croissant-

That once the thrill
of being alone has past,
our minds drift to our girls
and want to get home fast.

We think of how lonely
our lives would be,
that without our children
we wouldn't see.

How much happiness
it is being Mom and Dad
and how much joy
there is to be had.

As we walk the streets,
we find a window glass.
We see our reflection

both of us staring back.

We see a smiling couple
with no kids to be seen.
Looking relaxed and free
dressed up nice and clean.

We feel happy for them,
but deep down they know-
that real happiness isn't here,
they're waiting for us at home.

Quietly yours

We live in a world
where the loudest love
is the only one that matters.

But when it's just me and you
I'm quietly yours.

Right before I run naked into the ocean with my husband.

I want to seize
every moment
that awakes my soul
and reminds me that
I'm alive,
after sleep walking
through endless
daily routines.

Sunday mornings.

In your arms
I want to stay,
time won't know
to start the day.

Laying still
you can feel me breathe.
Please don't leave
please stay.

Fomo.

How do I live a life
where when I die,
I don't miss a thing?

Where I've lived it so fully,
that everything is satisfied?

Every part of me has been filled.

Every relationship has been full.
Every part of my body has been cherished.
Every choice has been embraced.
Every talent has been edified.
Every word has been said.
Every meal has been loved.
Every hour has been used.
Every moment has been savored.

How do I live a life
and not miss a thing?

Life.

To the stressed, it is a long life.
To the happy, it is a short life.
To the content, it is a simple life.
To the busy, it is a slaved life.

But to the grateful, it is a beautiful life.

Life after death.

The beautiful peony
that's worked so hard
to shine so brightly in life-
with all its colors and smells,

cut down, and arranged in a freshly watered vase
for everyone to admire still.

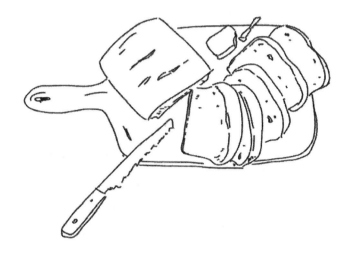

Is it mundane?

Is it really so mundane,
if it's the very foundation
of our life's existence?

Goodbyes.

I don't cry for the pain.
I don't cry for the loss.
I don't cry for the "never again's"
or the "last times."
For the "I wish we could haves"
or the "we didn't do's."

I cry for the joy it was to have had you.

For the love felt every day.
For the kindness shared.
For the hugs that were long.
For the laughs so hard.
For the longing to be together.

I cry for all the love.
For the overabundance of "love."

Melissa Elder lives on the east coast in Jersey with her husband and 2 girls amongst the trees. She loves the written word, and enjoys writing words too. *The Mundane* is her first book.

Made in the USA
Monee, IL
10 August 2023

47cf6afa-781e-4a87-8256-025361f10f27R01